WAR CRIMES

WAR CRIMES

·GOODW.Y.N·

atmosphere press

·Table of Contents·

Dedicated to Carmen Reyes, and her children.

Your absence is felt daily,

Your love is known eternally.

WAR
CRIMES

·Heathens·

The only writers of history left are the bastards erasing it.

·Spillage·

I promised myself that I would no

Longer write about the war.

Which one?

Iraq.

Afghanistan.

Yemen.

Syria.

Palestine.

Harlem.

Staten Island.

Chicago.

Ferguson.

Which one is it that haunts you the most?

All of them.

All of them.

All of them.

They all take the shape of the War I have

w/ myself. The war that keeps going with every breathe

I take. It rises like the phlegm in my throat, the bile in my stomach.

The words on this page.

I am NO LONGER afraid that no one will listen.

I am more afraid that the whole world is watching,

And I have nothing comfortable to say. No more compassion to give. Nothing to drive this beating heart, except for habit.

·Everybody here has PTSD.·

I

Everybody.

Here.

This America. Is a pit full of snakes!

We writhe and wiggle, withering and whining

Around each other's decaying bodies.

I see this motion daily in my mind's eye,

And shudder to think it truly so.

II

My white poet friends WRITE and rant and rave

About death as it is an inevitable thing, a visitor

That overstays a welcomed invitation. Whereas I

Have seen death in its cruelest forms and wondered

"How in the hell does PTSD affect those without affliction?"

When did the lives of civilians and soldiers and veterans intermingle,

Intertwine,

Intersect?

Then disperse and separate like a heat flash upon the clearest of skins.

III

I know, I know I am not making sense.

My words are of envy and that is something that is not meant to be understood.

I envy those with PTSD, who have no memories of warfare and—

Tanks, and barricades and usurping booby traps and nightmares of dropping bombs

And your face splattered against an aging brick wall that was once a palace.

·Rivers·

It keeps rolling in my head.

These houses of cards, built on borders

On the outskirts.

Nowhere to be found in the gentrification

Of the modern cities.

These jails, these prisons

These concentration camps are all the same.

They are jobs for the boys and girls in green.

Ordered to polish the sand with blood.

This is what we come home to.

A war wrapped in the arms of an empire—

Or starvation. Some of us dying in the streets

As I speak. In hushed tones of red, white, and blue.

What saved me?!

Maybe a zig; maybe a zag I dodged a bullet or two

Once or twice before. But you look at me as something

Honorable, something holy, something pure.

Please for the love of God DON'T.

DON'T THANK ME. FOR SERVICE.

Just don't. You have no idea of what it takes to

Run an empire; how bloody your hands get on what SERVICE

Will make you do.

Ask the guards at the prisons,

Ask the officers who run the camps.

Look them in the eyes and THANK THEM FOR YOUR SAFETY FROM GHOSTS.

·The Unholy Cabal·

I tried to write a poem about turtles once.

No. Yes—slightly.

The turtles were soldiers, our helmets

Were our shells.

I don't remember the rest.

Maybe it was about how we marched,

In slow cadences towards death.

Rhyme, rhythm can make heroes and slaves of us all.

One way or the other my best friends didn't like it.

"Too obvious," once dismayed.

"I know you can do better," grumbled another.

But this remnant is the closest I can come to a thing of beauty.

Even the disaster of a poem has been wiped from my mind's eye.

Except.

For one image.

Hatchlings crackling out of their eggs, slowly marching towards

The sea. You see I still see them—the turtles. Yet, I and other soldiers

Were never them.

We were/are the birds of prey who peck at the sands.

The silent killers.

The deadly ones.

·Flood Orange·

The old woman said to the police officer:

"Please don't tell me this…I cannot think,

I cannot breathe…I can do nothing."

She lost her breath after her second son

Was removed from the house. Will he be deported?

Just like her first?

"I can do nothing."

For me these are words on a sliver of paper.

Words that traveled in time, from page to print

To screen. Reaching into my heart and crushing it.

It has been almost 20 years since Iraq for me; I still

Long to go back there—to complete the story, see what

Survived, see what lays slowly dying by the wayside.

I am informed by many I SHOULDN'T GO BACK.

That there's nothing

To see. Truth is I still see Iraq every day. I suppose that is my

One true problem. The war for me never ended. It just expanded

Crossed oceans and seas, landed in cars, and fixed itself into
    driveways.

But who wants to hear that from a poet?

The very idea that I don't believe in goodness anymore is like

A knife in the back to someone somewhere.

And I can no longer divide, ICE from ISIS. Scandal from Scandal.

Word for word. Death for death, bomb for bomb, rumor from rumor.

It's all the same in my mind, one winding road to nowhere but hell.

·To Kill a Thirst in this Life·

I

Nestle©. Pure life...

I see this slogan now, every time I shut my eyes.

Every time I lift a plastic bottle to my face, I am still drinking you in

Life. This libation in memory of my memories. For those who
survived,

But like me are not quite fully here. I take you into me as if...

As if you were going out of style. As if you were my lifeline—as if

This was the last time I get to inhale you sucking you in through

Arid ivory teeth. I am tasting your perfected purification.

You are a river pouring...

Down, down, down-ranging past my tongue and cheek.

Into the heavy chasm of my aching throat.

"Ahh!" is all that I say. My thirst bubble busted, bent. Ran astray.

AWOL.

At least for another hour or so.

II

For me thirst is not an annoyance,

No, it is a nightmarish reminder. And unrelenting relinquishing of
time and space

And solace. It is a mouthful of salt in the morning. It is memories
    that greet me as

Kindly as scorpion stings. It is the ravenous buzzing of flies and
    mosquitos at high

Noon to 1800 hrs. If we were lucky. It is the trickling tease that
came from power suckling the mouth nub, connected to the
plastic tube, a vacuum that slurped* up the promise of cool,
refreshing water insulated, hiding from the harshness of OIF

Within our standard issued *CamelBaks©*.

CamelBak©--all distributed, each decorated uniformly in
matching fabrications of Arabian Desert landscape: camouflage
facets of bold tans, pale greens, and bleached greys. All three
colors frosted seemed faded. Like Polaroid© photographs, spat out
of time, now unflappable remnants—polar ice caps left to melt
slowly by the sun.

I store them in the back of my boxed-up brain; the sunburns that
I gained, maintained—kept the pain of that amongst other things
to myself. And for 9 months out of 12, I have succeeded mostly
in avoiding them. And yet there are inhabitants now.

Skeletons, and demons that venture out on previous to October.

It seems for them to be too stuffy in there. Hell is hot; these devils
    demand their ice water.

And so, my All Hallows Eve begins in June.

By July, the city and I—we are both boiling.

Stirred and stewed by Lucifer's breath—his blistered bellow, his red
    face beaming.

It makes no goddamn sense, when you are the nonsense, you can
    never escape.

So, I sit with the enemy which is myself. My body—98.6 degrees.
    The molten lava that is existing in the here and now.

Knowing full well that most will never get it. War is like packing
sand just to bring to the beach.

At the end of the day, conversations that recall my adventurous
misadventures annoy most with pictures of glory—and their
white-lit patriotism, both rattles and ransacks me.

So, I would rather talk about something, less distracting.

"How's the weather?"

"Hot," I say.

"What was it like in Iraq?"

"Hot," I say.

Truth be told it was more than just. Their faces, the Iraqi people
float to me.

Men, and women, and children lost. Fervent grains of sand falling
within an eternal hourglass.

— Images. They are waves upon waves approaching the shores of
my waking mind. And with a snap, they slip away just as quickly
as they came. But the guilt, the guilt that always remains.

Never gone. Never clean. My body shakes, I take another drink.
First in sips then gulps. Will I ever be free?

It hurts too much to cry; so, I don't. I don't...I have to preserve
what little purity I have left. *Nestle©?* Where are you *Nestle©?*
No more bottles to spare? No more wares to peddle me?

When I was a little girl, I thought that lifelike love was peace—
and peace was the milky taste of chocolate that lingered upon my
lips. Inside my mouth, melting on my tongue, against the fleshy
pink of my cheeks. Staining my hollow insides coffee brown—
much darker than my outer skin. I could tell the difference
between the shades of those two.

Now pure life it seems you have abandoned my sight. I see the
Iraqi children—destitute, hovering over rubble, starving for food,
bellies rumble like thunder. But for them there was never any

rain. No rain, no water—no purity to make their lives clean again. Couldn't tell what their real complexions were under all that filth. Lost my mind some days back then—wondered if it really was that we are all just born dirty.

The heat itself was always as thick as molasses but never as sweet. In my own perspiration, I drowned every single day. In it still I have drowned every single day since. The only reality I have now is that I am hot; I am dehydrating, I need food, cold water, a lukewarm bath. I need to be always clean—I need to always be hydrated.

And if I slip…well.

That's when it screams at me.

The wild will to live it hollers non-stop until the paranoid alarm

Is shattered. Its fire doused out silenced.

III

"Drink water! Beat the heat, beat the heat!"

Except, I know this release is temporary.

Conditioning—brainwashing…Military training can only do so much.

Nothing now saves me from the truth of the truth. There is nothing PURE about survival.

It is all a routine. A balance beam to hold the mission together. As long as we followed orders

We lived. The roof, the roof, the roof was always on fire: We just kept drinking water so it won't

Burn AND cave us all in. So, we did as told "hydrate or die, hydrate or die, hydrate…"

But still all of us die, died, are dying anyway.

But… My greatest fear isn't dying, it is that I have ingested so much "Life,"

That all I can do now IS LIVE.

Its power is stored in my undying cells.

I'm the goddamned *Energizer©* bunny.

I'll just keep going and going and going…

Outliving every decent thing.

An empty privilege. It robs me of my goodness—

I am so rancid with anger at surviving, I've forgotten how good it can be to live.

·Beating Drums·

I

There's a pounding

A rattling inside my skull.

My headaches again.

A fire that touches against the grey matter

And I am stolen in pain.

I wonder if it's the inheritance that the ancestors give.

The jewel of my blackness carved into my flesh.

The fury they carried in their silence. Their backs never

Bending like mines. How did their hearts beat under the pressure?

II

I've been fighting for my life

All my life. Stabbing at the demons

That have faces like mine. Voices like mine.

Shadows that steal the meaning from my life.

That pollutes the air I breathe. And wander this earth

Like the living dead. Simultaneously soulless and light—

w/o my own body.

·Change your taste·

I find myself afraid of men these days.

The way they sweat and grunt a strange lot.

Nothing coming out of their mouths of tenderness.

Nothing soft in their hands anymore, as they reach for

My neck or my back or my ass.

No caress. Not gentleness. None.

I have been a friend to men most of my life and I have

Also been so deep in trenches that they forget I am a woman.

Well, some do. Others expose themselves when willing to fuck,

And I am tired, y'all.

Of hiding from men in my apartment. Somewhere in NYC.

Somewhere in Harlem. Somewhere where it's quiet and I

Can fill my lungs with air and just…

WOOOOOOOOOOO. Because men have their ways.

Their ways to invade…

S   P   A   C   E

My daughter, my daughter I can see it in her eyes.

She fears men too. The way they speak these days

So rough and frightening, the way they need to stomp

While entering the room. You know these men—all too well.

And I'm not saying all, and I am not saying some I'm saying MEN.

Yes. I'm finally saying it: that you have beaten the fear into my body,

Into my bones, into my soul and you know why I cannot lay with
   you again.

And we laugh and we joke, and I smile, and I am choking on these
different sensations

And no, I don't need your good dick as the cure. Or a hug, or you
just trying to be nice.

Or maybe I do. I don't know what I need. I don't know what I'll
need to take away this pain! But

I am starting with the following. Admittance. Admitting not omitting
yes. Yes, I am these days I

am afraid of men.

·The Tranquil Fires in the Boat·

The fireworks explode like distant mortar rounds.

The light bouncing high into the air never descends to earth again.

It is only I trapped w/ this cage,

Carved out of my own flesh and silent tears.

As the audience collects along the shore

dumbfounded; the flickers began to flourish within the boat.

As the emptiest seashells scattered decorating the beach.

My mind is buried in the sands a million years past and away

Where the celebrations were not so friendly for, they cherished war and nurtured death

And the people's eyes held what was embodied in them, shock
             awe   fear

For we had hard-bludgeoned it into their heads, similar to how we plug the pledge of allegiance fresh into a child's mind

Soldier and death had become one in the same

As for the rest of America, it celebrates its liberation.

I am not of the stock that feels proud.

I am not of the trade that feels liberated.

I am the shadow behind the American flag, when it is half-masted and mostly forgotten

Every other day of the week.

·Death to All Falsehoods!·

Rid me of the middlemen!

Tear me from the mainstream!

Bleed me of all symbols,

Entangle me to the real thing!

·Do not go to War·

Do not go to war.

Do not go to war, in the name of the dead.

Do not go to war in the dawn of an Old flame,

Its embers draped in the rains of blood, blessed by fear.

The fear of mothers and fathers,

The fear of children,

Yours and mine.

We are all taught in this modern world now,

To fear such gifts. The darkness, the unknowable.

The silent clicks and pauses of tongues,

Eruptions of emotions, buildings collapsing.

Walls crumbling. We are all taught to fear.

We are taught to believe in fear,

Worship in fear, parade, and praise in boasts

To be greater conquerors and concur with the

Domination, the brave besting of fear.

But we never win. Fear wins. It concurs us,

When instead of extending hands,

We exchange arms. Instead of realizing that,

In all that armor we are still afraid.

Aye...I.

I know the sound of drums.

I still hear the wail of sorrow. Mothers, young, old

It matters not. They all bury their sons in the end.

Hopes, dreams. It's funny how all these things become superfluous,

Once you are dead.

Fathers, sisters we are left with the sanity of the insane.

Those victims we march in the name of we all executed.

Black lives, white cops. It doesn't matter to them anymore.

They are all dead. I suppose that is true equality.

They have all come to me,

They ask of me to tell the world,

One thing.

They say, "Tell them, tell them not to duel in our names."

I will say: "The world will not listen. Most will curse me for saying,

The slain black children, and those murdered cops are the same now and forever the same."

They say, tell them anyway.

TELL THEM ANYWAY.

I sigh.

Do not use their names.

They do not care for it, even if, especially if you cry justice.

Our vengeance will not make us immortal.

We will not be saints.

Our rage,

Their rage.

We are two bulls clashing, in the end.

For what?

Bloodshed comforts no one.

Only remembrance.

·It's the End·

I

My daughter plays REM and laughs.

Michael Stipes' melodious voice bellows out

"It's the end of the world as we know it…"

And a sadness fills my body. Quickly.

I suppose it is my heart breaking, again.

How unfair life is. I have seen the end of the world

Before, while in Iraq in 2003. That summer I will never forget.

Seeing homes and buildings blown apart, as if they were hungry
   mouths.

Removed of all teeth,

Wide open and empty. Except for the families. Those like us in
   quarantine.

A scorpion and a camel-spider in jars amusing ourselves to death

w/ little cuts and jabs. Trying to hold

On to a shred of humanity. While several years later my daughter
   laughs to cover up her

Fear. And I am so tired of living through apocalypses. Of seeing the
   pieces topple, of empires

Falling and crushing only the poorest of souls first.

When is the end the end? Or are these stories part of a whole new
   beginning?

How can I raise up the children to smile as if tomorrow is promised
   then?

II

I still stare at my daughter's scars.

They lay on her right arm, slashes—violent slashes as if she escaped some

Jason-based horror. Tell me again gurl, why cut into yourself?

Tell me again gurl...   Y LIE?

Is this how you deal with Armageddon? By hating yourself?

Is this the price of first-world privileges?

And I slide of venom pierces through my lips.

"If I can *survive* the crack-era, she sure as hell can *SURVIVE THIS!*"

And I realize survival requires your heart to grow a little cold. Just a little.

Just   a fuckin'   little.

·Now who's laughing·

We soldiers used to make fun of the hadjis for NOT using toilet paper.

For washing their left hand, and only their left hand—which was used to wipe

Their assess.

Never did it occur to many that the Persians invented the toilets. While the

English were still using outhouses.

And today as I stare at my stock of Angel Soft, this memory bubbles upward.

COVID-19 will make pulpers of us all.

·Raccoon Eyes·

Look friend. The friendless walk a long way to nowhere. Now here

I am wasting away from walking *y'alllll*, back-bent slouches w/o
footprints for

A legacy.

A pot full of piss and regrets, a life unseen.

Barely one worth noticing. Chasing dreamscapes and getting out of
others' way.

Lying flat like white paste adoring silver silencers, cold wooden gears
cascading over

A metal winter.

The juices boiled overcut and daunting task force left to fill in God's
worth

By way of mouth. Only I can search for a self,

Lost in selfies.

·Upon the Stairs·

In front of you I cried.

With tears, brokenness.

Back-bent, shoulders slouched.

From time spent trudging the weight of

The Earth.

I wept on bended knee, each droplet

Salting the concrete.

I yelped at the future horrors, before they

Revealed their inhuman faces.

You witness this upon the stairs,

And show my pandemonium, no mercy.

Through the glistening stream I could see you

Laughing at my weakness.

Upon the stairs your feet stood

Above it all; towering.

·Wakanda Forever·

Dearest Universe,

> Deliver me unto Wakanda. A paradise where
> when
>
> Black women are raped, we are Believed.

·The Differing Reasons·

I

Once upon a time, I was not the master of my own fate.

My life was in the hands of my mother and stepfather and yes

Those hands, those hands at times were very, very cruel.

But neither were they the masters of their own fates. They were molded

And shaped by the oppression of their parents, and their parents, parents, and so on.

This pain carried in the blood. Hereditary.

II

It was a house afraid to love.

I grew w/this knowledge—early.

It costed me my childhood.

It was a death, a small death but a death nonetheless.

III

I am sometimes in love with death.

In my wounded heart, I have had to fight to love myself.

My heart is still a Brooklyn Bound J train, hustling

through the darkness

Aimlessly.

IV

I will not lie.

The desert calls to me.

It is always calling.

There are some sunsets in those places,

Blood red and sweet.

w/ oceans possessed w/ so much life.

V

If you wish to keep a secret,

Even from yourself—especially from yourself

Whisper it to a silverback gorilla.

Trust me, they are lovely because they dare not speak.

VI

Some days, some nights, sometimes I am lonely.

I cannot forgive or forgive you. You, you, all of you!

And death, the sweetest love of my life tends to lie

In my ears. In slow hushed whispers:

Come with me and I will let you finally sleep.

·3,2,1·

I

And so goes the blast off

Those granted the permission to dream

Leaving behind the rest to rot

I wonder if there is a God up there

Has he his arms now only opened for the rich?

II

You climbed for money

And good fortune

And now the atmosphere

Presses against you too tightly

Here

So, you aspire for more

While paying no taxes,

And I can't blame you for that,

I blame you instead for

Leaving the workers with brittle hands

Blistered and bruised, eyelids chaffed

to drown in

Their own sweat, and blood

While pounding back the need to piss

On themselves

So, they can pay the bill collectors on time.

III

We who have the vaccine and a choice

Are not lucky, but privileged beyond belief

While the rest of the world gurgles on its snot and tears

Their inconsolable cries for their loved ones

While loved ones are burned, their bodies

Charred to stop the spread

Until another variant comes along

To wash away the efforts of those in hospital

Smocks, gowns, and latex gloves

Who forego rest endlessly, for work without sleep.

Some of us are ungrateful as would be

A party of

Spoiled three-year-olds.

Who've forgotten what it's like to feel real pain

And loss when they receive a Black pony instead of a White

horse.

·Hammerman:
A Poem about D. Rumsfeld·

I say I don't wanna be yo' tool no mo'.

I say I don't wanna be yo' tool no mo'.

Too much blood on mah Black hands.

Too much blood on mah Black hands.

I look in her eyes and see she already dead

From the time she been bore 'til now.

Yo' stole her heart,

Yo' ate it raw.

Yo' stole her soul,

Drank it down slow.

I don't wanna be yo' tool no mo'.

I don't wanna be yo' tool no mo'.

Hammerman, he long been dead!

'Cept the memories of his voice

in mah head!

HATE CRIMES

·The Ballad of Botham Jean & Atatiana Jefferson·

I

There is an agony inside of me

Boxed in and shuttered down

My eyes vacant yet full of tears

Revolving around a one-word question: Why?

II

They were shot in their houses.

They were shot in their houses.

They were shot in their houses.

They were shot in their houses.

They were shot in their houses.

Within their own fuckin' abode...

Nowhere is safe. Not even home.

·Inner Mouthbites·

I'm afraid to step foot into

My mother's house.

There is a lie playin' deeply

On my tongue.

Scars that nibble and grip

the shit out of the insides of

my cheeks.

Bones refusing to stay buried.

Every time she asks:

How Shylah? How's my granddaughter doing?

I grit my teeth into a pain staked

Smile: She's just fine mama, she's just fine.

·Even the Best Swimmers Drown·

I

Water, water everywhere

None to drink

But plenty to drown in.

II

Her favorite pastime became

A vehicle

That she almost ended her life with.

III

On this day,

At this God-given moment

I discovered

How much self-hatred my 16-year-old

daughter

Has inherited.

·Respect for the Dead II (Slumbering) ·

I see the sleeping homeless man

Alone

In the train station waiting room

Dedicated to the fallen, dead

Soldiers forgotten by time.

·At War w/Words·

My friend Beau said something interesting about how

Evil men speak about "others":

THE BLACKS.

THE JEWS.

THE MUSLIMS,

THE MEXICANS,

THE GAYS...

Enough emphasis to separate and divide.

Walls, walls, and more walls as if our

Very own words betray our souls.

Am I screaming into the void for nothing?

·Bated Breath·

The girl on the TV said that she felt

"Safe" to worship in the city, especially here

As if New York had somehow changed and

Been freed from prejudice. For Hanukah, I wished

Them merriment.

Mirth.

A day when ignorance wouldn't reach the synagogue.

But what am I to know?

I am one of the many who sits on her ass, and

Enjoys the crash.

·Excessive Clutter·

I

I often dreamed of dying

While my apartment was a horde

Of trash. I dreamt that the floors were

Clean and that they would find my body

Sitting against the refrigerator door. Upright,

Wrists slit. Blood red—my body grey, and everything

Else in the apartment would be empty. Save the walls.

They would be gleaming white.

II

I read the obituary of Ms. Joy Noel, 85.

Evicted into the cold; excuse me a nursing home

Away from family and friends, nestled somewhere

In the cruel heart of this unforgiving city.

·POPSmoke·

I

We bury the youth suddenly,

As if we have no courage for the future at all.

II

1 mo' again

1 mo' again

1 mo' again

1 mo' again

1 mo' again

1 mo' again…

·Dear Toni·

--For Toni Morrison

Is death a vagrant thing?

We come away with your words;

Your works etched on our flesh, body, and bone.

I cannot remember the times I was touched—moved

Removed from pain.

Yet you kept screaming for us, to us, by us

To be heard.

Like a hungry ghost.

A dog with a slab of meat; ravenous to the core.

I let myself go, just to hear your voice in my ears.

Crack open the sky for me mama.

I'm flying to you. Flying home.

·Dawn the Blood I Cough Up·

Yesterday, I woke up and realized

That after the war,

I am still screaming inside my own throat.

LOVE
CRIMES

·Breaking Bread·

I

These are the hours I dread the most;

No one believes me when I say,

I know when the sun comes up.

I can feel the chill in my bones--till this day.

When one half of the world, turns

to sleep and the other rises.   its other self a crescent moon

awaken and yet...

Not.

II

The desert never sleeps; never

ceases to whisper.   Once it calls

your name, it will never stop pulling

you into its waters.

A great womb that leaves you divided

Your soul   split from body,

Like a hazel cat's eye.

This, the beautiful, lonely hell

I return to its hungry belly daily.

Its barren taste,   a dashing salt kiss

Is a parting gift left

By the ghosts that are too mine.

III

These old hands that can crush my breasts,

Why are they so gentle?

Why do they choose   to caress

me instead?

IV

I only know of dawn, as a remnant.

A fracture,   a haunting of stories

lost in sand, inscribed across

time of space   love letters written in blood

V

The long-standing savoring of honey;

the tender touch of dates, fed into a hungry

mouth. So young, too foolish to know that

the best things in life are perishable, all the while

possessing memories everlasting.

·Sweat·

Bury me so deep inside your

Wicked cave

Open to me and I will kill this drought

And drown your desert in rains

So luscious, so pure

·Visitors·

I

I am myself

Low crawling through the dust

Being engulfed by sanded fog.

The drama of being lost underneath

The giant's foot of sky, blue sparks

Reflected in blackness pools of soot, soothe

My taste for the blood-orange fires that storm

And thunder

Within my mind.

II

My mind cradled a thunderstorm,

Bombs kabooming for hours on end,

The sound like tires crossing over manned

Manholes. Bridges cloak and cover droppings; claymores of

Opinions spilling on overnight

Exiled children that time forgave and then forgot.

And me with my rifle in hand

Going toe-to-toe w/ death. A deal breaker was my exodus.

III

If I were to return to Iraq, I'd wish

Foes to welcome me with arms

Not arms in blooded rust-soiled hands, arms that once knew

Combatants embraces riddled w/ the puzzlement,

Demise drenched dreams drained showers in July bring

Forth only hear independent of mercy.

·Respect for the Dead·

I

They mourned 9/11 in the city again

Today. I passed by the article, forgetting

To leer at the pictures of the attendants, the mourners

The morning was darkness cloudy, bellies fat w/expecting rain

As if the pain was still too heavy for the city to carry on its own.

Or is it rather, the memory of pain? When I bore my *first—only* child

I remember the blood, the birth, the silence…but not the pain. And that

Is the crux of it. The memory of pain fades; all that is left is longing.

II

This was supposed to be a poem about 9/11.

About death. I forgot the original words to the stanzas

Though. My thoughts drifted; I fell asleep.

I dreamt of the crystals in the soldiers' lungs. Tubes clogged

With titanium and iron, precious metals stealing the air right

From their nostrils. No one mourns these men, these women—not yet.

Please not another thanks. I am too tired to remember why the war

Was fought. Why we lost what was lost. Time. Limbs. Air. Space;

Sleep. Sleep. And moreover, rest. I almost feel that the nation mourns

For the build alone. The collapse of the twins. But not those left in
the desert

Or

the mountains. Not us. When the lights go out, and the day is done,
no one truly

Thanks the janitor for cleaning up the day's mess.

III

One day my daughter's daughters will ask me about 9/11.

And I will say that is when it truly all fell apart.

·Feral·

Not all things buried are dead.

Not all things dead are buried.

The half of you that outgrew the animal

Has grown back with fuller teeth.

You bite down hard. Just for comfort

For shelter. You taste my flesh against

Your pinkish tongue.

Are you half cat my dear?

This I keep wondering.

I can't put my finger on why, but you

Were born something wild.

Even in a box.

Even in a cage.

There is something about you

Closer to free…

·Untitled #1·

In these days I do feel

Slightly

Under

Yet I want to take this time

To say, to feel, to write

Something happy…

In this short while my daughter GROWS

And the sun shines brighter

Chasing away the cold

I am hopeful that both she,

The spring and my very own words

Shall outlive the twilight.

·Untitled #2·

My childhood invoked great sadness in me

Almost like a grave

A deep hole to cover in darkness

Nothingness and empty silence

Why should I smile then?

Carrying all those years upon my brow.

A weight upon my head that

till this day never ceases, nor fades

I smile because of you and only you

Dear child!

You were a crack in the cycle

A hole in the world

A heartbeat next to mine

That made happiness, shelter

Warmth possible.

And as I break away from this world

In due time yours is a name

Etched upon my soul

Forever, ever, and ever beyond

In your eyes I have been born

A child against the will of those

Who torched my skin w/ indifference?

I humbly thank you little mother

Forever and ever and ever still

Always.

·Beautiful Strangers·

I read somewhere that they're

Going to rename a park in Brooklyn

After Marsha P. Johnson. For some this

Must be happy news for her to be remembered

In such a way. So why am I so saddened? I feel

It in my bones—another martyr another effigy.

Something greater than a life's work, but…

Less than a life. We say our hellos and goodbyes

To them throughout the years; while the memory of

The person fades.

Somewhere in my mind I am dying too. And

I cry out SAVE ME DAMN IT!!!!! But all I get back is,

That must have been hard on you. Keep on doing the right

Thing for you and your daughter. But I tell you what is the right

Thing? Pills? Being locked away?

For our own safety I am told. But how is it that when no one listens

To your cries that is the safest thing?

A long time ago I thought I was Jesus, and that answered everything

And nothing. I guess the role is a hand-me-down in history that is
continuous,

And must be played.

·These Days·

Since my daughter has tried to

Kill herself, twice a week, I have to let the social worker in.

Twice a week, I have to let the social worker in.

Twice a week, I have to let the social worker in.

My life has become a bag of bullshit, spun on routine.

Just to save her life and she is ungrateful to this sacrifice.

I know it.

I want to go back to the days when I wrote about flowers.

But there are no flowers right now; even though this is a "hot" winter.

I have no faith in these words.

The war rages inside of me and I am angry at other poets who lack their rage.

"Where is it?!"

"Where is it?!"

"Where is it?!"

Nowhere else.

It's all mine.

And that ladies and gentlemen, is the beauty and the horror of it.

·Am I fittin' to Love a Black Man? ·

I

And Him shout aloud " I LOVVVVVEE WHITE WOMEN!!!!!"

Him be dark-skinned, him be a Black man.

Him be right in front of I, and I see through.

Him be talented. Him be not rough in stuff; him be a Black man.

I be see through.

II

And she say with open arms:

"Dey not lookin' at us!" Her with full-figure

Big gal, light-skinned eyes beautify shade of hazel green.

Her bosom opened to mine, like a half-cut watermelon scoop

Out da heart and get to the meat of the problem. "Dey not lookin' for us!"

I be open wide dat day an' angry dat her be chasin' dem reminds I of self

In clauses and perhaps and wishin' wishin' and maybe's along with if only.

·Mirza·

That evening while sharing coffee,

I was too afraid to be myself.

Beauty is your business it seems;

Perfection an obsessive goal.

When you said you were into minds,

I figured you a liar. Because all the bodies

They were wrapped up in looked similar if not

The same.

Skinny, little things—women, younger

Than you or I. Caught your eye, and kept your thoughts

On them, with them in mind.

"Why should I bear my soul then?" What I thought meant

For the night, has become a pretense.

I hate to admit these words, I've been buried deeply ever since.

·Nina's Violent Song·

I

I said what I said to the small

Crowd of Queer Black chilens,

"Are you ready to smash White things!"

And they knew what I meant, the rally

Cry for freedom, thick like the sweat

Sticking to their backsides.

II

What I wouldn't give for a gun that

Shot roses instead of bullets

Fragrance in the air of petals in the rain

Instead of Black man's ash and blood.

I wonder if White men fear being left

In the sun to bleed out and die,

The way we fear the truth as we bear

Witness to those who already had.

·Casablanca·

I thought this the richest place for romance on earth

The idea of the Arabic sands against my skin made my

Hairs stand up

The brisk African air caressing my breasts…

I cannot lie it awakened the beast in me,

Desire for a man, for entrance, for penetration

Into the soul's soul. The one which slumbered for

So long that I forgot that I was a woman who once

Demanded things, for herself and her only, her own body

alone.

·About Atmosphere Press·

Atmosphere Press is an independent, full-service publisher for excellent books in all genres and for all audiences. Learn more about what we do at atmospherepress.com.

We encourage you to check out some of Atmosphere's latest releases, which are available at Amazon.com and via order from your local bookstore:

·About the Author·

Nicole Goodwin aka GOODW.Y.N. is the author of *Warcries*, as well as the *2020 Pushcart Nominee, 2018-2019 Franklin Furnace Fund Recipient,* the *2018 Ragdale Alice Judson Hayes Fellowship Recipient, 2017 EMERGENYC Hemispheric Institute Fellow* as well as the *2013- 2014 Queer Art Mentorship Queer Art Literary Fellow.* She published the articles "Talking with My Daughter…" and "Why is this Happening in Your Life…" in the New York Times' parentblog *Motherlode.* Additionally, her work "'Desert Flowers" was shortlisted and selected for performance by the *Women's Playwriting International Conference* in Cape Town, South Africa in 2015.